Welles-Turner Memorial Library

a department of the Town of Glastonbury

Glastonbury, Connecticut

Cornelia H. Nearing

Memorial Collection

Corneila H. Nearing (1871-1959) was a fine artist and a great citizen of Glastonbury. She loved and used our library and was a great believer in sharing resources. The citizens of Glastonbury continue to enjoy the benefits of her generosity through an endowment she established for the Library. It is from those resources that this book has been purchased for your use and enjoyment.

The Cape Cod
Christmas
Cookbook

written by
Mark Jasper

illustrated by
Holly Shaker

On
Cape Publications

Cape Cod, Massachusetts

Edited by Adam Gamble & Stuard Derrick.

Interior book design and production by DMAC.
E-mail: dmac@mts.net
Cover design and production by Joe Gallante, Coy's Brook Studio.
E-mail: coysbrookstudio@comcast.net

ISBN: 0-9719547-6-3

For more information please contact:

On Cape Publications
Toll free: 1-877-662-5839
On the web at: www.oncapepublications.com
E-mail: chef@oncapepublications.com

First edition.

10 9 8 7 6 5 4 3 2 1

Printed in Canada.

Acknowledgements

First and foremost, I owe a debt of gratitude to my wife, Sharon, for all her help and support. I would personally like to thank my mother, Marilyn Jasper, who helped out tremendously with this book. I would also like to thank my sister, Rachel Boylestad, and my father, Michael Jasper, for sharing their wonderful recipes. Special thanks to Mary Sicchio of Cape Cod Community College, my good friend Jean Gardner from Tales of Cape Cod, and Earl Mills, Sr., owner of the Flume Restaurant and author of the Cape Cod Wampanoag Cookbook. Last but not least, I'd like to thank my publisher, Adam Gamble, and my editor, Stuard Derrick.

For Sharon and Hannah.

Cape Cod Christmas Menu

Main Courses and Side Dishes

Desserts

Christmas Brunch

Introduction

"Whosoever shall be found observing any such day as Christmas, or the like, either by forbearing labor, feasting, or any other way upon such account as aforesaid, every such person so offending shall pay for each offense five shillings as a fine to the country," stated the Massachusetts law of 1659. Christmas was a bitter reminder of the religious persecution the Pilgrims had to endure by the Church of England, and why they had to escape.

Much has changed since the 17th century, yet this little cranberry-laden corner of New England, known as Cape Cod, has somehow managed to elude time. From its historic villages to its well-preserved sea captain's homes, the Cape looks very much as it did centuries ago.

Throughout my early childhood days, I used to dream of what it would be like to spend Christmas on Cape Cod. My family used to summer here; but as soon as the frigid north wind began to rattle the shutters, it was back to dreary Worcester, Massachusetts, where I was born and most of my family resided.

I was about three years of age when my small hands first touched a piece of sticky bread dough. My grandfather used to prop me up on the wooden workbench at his bakery whenever I would visit. As I began to get a little older, I was allowed to assist the bakers. Sometimes it was nothing more than emptying baskets of piping hot rolls into the bins in the front of the store, or just sweeping off the floury workbench. But no matter how menial the task, I always performed it with great pride.

For most children, the day before Christmas was a time for wrapping gifts, putting the finishing touches on the Christmas tree, or frolicking in the snow. But for me, it meant rising at the crack of dawn, frantically putting on my old clothes, and shaking my poor mother out of bed so she could drive me to the bakery. This was the one day of the year when I worked harder than a steel-mill worker and had more fun than any child had a right to. My grandfather would be at his best (or worst, some might argue). His face would turn many different shades of red; and of course, he would scream at most anything that moved. The first time I attempted to take the rolls out of the oven by myself, I immediately heard, "What are you doing? Look at these rolls! They're not baked enough. They're going to fold up like an accordion. Put them back in the oven!", he shouted. This was followed by my grandmother's low but firm voice as she addressed my grandfather, "Sammy, I'd like to see you in the office now." It took me every bit of strength to keep the tears from flowing. Please understand, my grandfather and I had the most wonderful relationship; but if you were in the bakery wearing an apron, you were fair game. No longer in the bakery business, I look back on those days with the fondest of memories, particularly around Christmas time.

When I began gathering recipes for this cookbook, many a chef asked why I chose to write this particular type of book. Unquestionably, my inspiration came from my childhood, but I also wanted to share with the world some great family recipes. It's probable that if some of my family were still alive and knew I was giving out their secret recipes, they would have me beheaded, but that's a story for another day.

Being fortunate enough to have been able to move to the Cape in 1996, I now understand why people travel from across the globe to spend Christmas on this narrow spit of land. To stroll its antique villages during the holidays is like falling into a Charles Dickens novel. The echoes of Christmas carolers can be heard on every street corner. Shops are busy handing out Christmas cookies and hot cider to their patrons. And houses are decorated in the most magical ways. Cape Codders seem to smile just a little more this time of year. They know that Christmas is more than gift giving or tree trimming; they also know it's about feasting, Cape Cod style. Walk into any good cook's kitchen around the holidays and your senses will be overcome with delight. The smell of fresh seafood will permeate the air. You will undoubtedly hear the sounds of Wellfleet oysters being shucked, brilliant red lobster claws being cracked, and Chatham sea clams being popped open, all turned into extraordinary chowders and savory seafood dishes. Fresh vegetables will be prepared and transformed into delicious, creative side dishes or rich, luscious bisques. And of course, the versatile cranberry will be used to create the tastiest of sauces, yummy pies, and delectable cakes. Ask any honest Cape Codder and they will tell you Christmas on Cape Cod is all about food.

Within this book you will find recipes from the finest kitchens on Cape Cod. From incredible drinks to the most decadent desserts, these holiday recipes will please the most fickle of palates. If you live on the Cape or at least have spent a December 25th or two here, you are one of the lucky ones. But even if you come from someplace far away and cannot be a part of the Christmas celebration, let the finest chefs of

Cape Cod and their glorious recipes follow you back to wherever home may be. And may these wonderful recipes make your holiday just a little more special.

"Merry Christmas to all and to all, a good night!"

Holiday Drinks

Creamy Rich Eggnog

Captain Ezra Nye Bed & Breakfast
Sandwich, MA

"I call this 'creamy, rich,' but it only appears and tastes that way. Only 1/4 to 1/2 pint whipping cream is used. The egg whites, beaten stiff, make it seem rich." – Elaine Dickson

This recipe comes from Elaine's mother. Elaine Dickson and her husband, Harry were the former owners of the Captain Ezra Nye B & B.

Ingredients:

2 quarts whole milk
1 cup sugar
1/3 cup flour
4 eggs, separated
2 teaspoons vanilla
nutmeg
1 teaspoon sugar per egg
1/4 to 1/2 pint whipping cream

With whisk, blend sugar and flour in a large saucepan. Add milk gradually, whisking to combine. Cook on medium heat, whisking constantly, to boiling. Boil one minute, stirring. Remove from heat. Whisk egg yolks thoroughly in a small bowl, then pour some of the hot milk mixture in and combine. Return milk mixture to the stove, and add egg mixture, whisking constantly. Cook until it comes to a boil, and let boil for one minute. Remove from heat and cool.

Beat egg whites until stiff, adding 1 teaspoon sugar per egg. Add eggnog. The eggnog is like a custard, it's so thick.

Chill. When ready to serve, add whipping cream and sprinkle with nutmeg.

Serves 10 – 12.

Hot Cranberry Punch

Thornton W. Burgess Museum
Sandwich, MA

Ingredients:

2 cups sugar
1 cup water
1 cup lemon juice
4 cups cranberry juice

4 cups pineapple juice
1/2 teaspoon cinnamon
1/2 teaspoon ginger
lemon slices studded with cloves

Boil sugar and water over medium heat for 10 minutes. Add lemon, cranberry and pineapple juices and spices. Heat slowly until just boiling. Cool slightly; pour into a warmed punch bowl. Garnish with lemon slices studded with cloves.

This punch has been served during several Christmas events at the Thornton W. Burgess Museum in Sandwich Village.

Serves 20 – 4-ounce servings.

Christmas Beach Plum Rum

Ingredients:

1 quart beach plum berries
1 cup sugar
rum

Place beach plum berries in a bottle. Add the cup of sugar and fill bottle with rum, making sure to cap off the bottle. This drink should be made during the late summer and allowed to age until Christmas. The bottle should be rotated frequently until opened.

Lemon Liqueur

Bramble Inn & Restaurant
Brewster, MA
Chef/Owner Ruth Manchester

"We love to make this lovely liqueur right after Thanksgiving to give as gifts on Christmas. We funnel it into pretty sterilized bottles with stoppers from The Christmas Tree Shop. It is always well received. Good to make a little extra to have on hand for company." — Ruth

Ingredients:

3 cups vodka
1 cup sugar
2 cups water
zest from 4 lemons

Put zest in 2 cups vodka and set aside for 3 days. Bring water and sugar to a boil and cool. Add syrup to lemon vodka mixture with remaining cup of vodka. Store at least 36 hours.

Holiday Hot Chocolate

19th Hole Tavern
Hyannis, MA

Ingredients:

1 ounce Peppermint Schnapps
1/2 ounce Butterscotch
Schnapps
1 cup hot chocolate

Mix and serve.

Hot Chocolate and Rum

19th Hole Tavern
Hyannis, MA

Ingredients:

1 ounce Captain Morgan Rum
1/2 ounce Butterscotch
Schnapps
1 cup hot chocolate

Mix and serve.

Candy Manor Hot Chocolate

Chatham Candy Manor
Chatham, MA

Ingredients:

3 ounces unsweetened chocolate, grated
1/3 cup boiling water
1 quart milk, warmed
1/3 cup sugar
1 teaspoon ground cinnamon
1 teaspoon peppermint extract

Pour the milk into a saucepan; add the sugar and heat until steaming hot, stirring frequently. Place the chocolate in a medium saucepan and melt over hot water. Gradually add the boiling water to the melted chocolate, stirring with a stiff wire whisk or a hand-held electric mixer, until smooth in consistency. Stir in the sweetened, warm milk; whisk mixture over low heat until steaming. Remove from heat and add the cinnamon and peppermint extract. Serve with a dollop of homemade whipped cream.

<u>Whipped Cream:</u>
8 ounces heavy cream
2 tablespoons confectioners' sugar
1/4 teaspoon vanilla extract
2 tablespoons crushed candy cane

Chill the cream until it is very cold. Chill the mixing bowl in the freezer. Pour the cream into the mixing bowl; add the sugar and vanilla extract. Whip until the cream forms soft peaks. Fold in the crushed candy canes.

Note: It is best to use an electric mixer to whip the cream.

Serves 4 – 6.

Admiral's Cider

The British Beer Company
Falmouth, MA

Ingredients:

1½ ounces spiced rum
6-8 ounces hot apple cider

Mix rum and hot apple cider in a glass mug. Rim mug with cinnamon
and sugar. Top with whipped cream and a cinnamon stick.

Christmas Coffee

19th Hole Tavern
Hyannis, MA

Ingredients:

1½ ounces Bailey's
Irish Crème
1 cup black coffee
whipped cream

Mix and serve with
whipped cream.

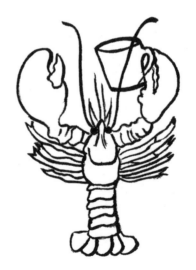

Appetizers and Soups

Lobster Cheesecake

Christian's Restaurant
Chatham, MA
Executive Chef Don Dickerson

Ingredients:

1 cup dry Parmesan cheese
1 cup Italian crumbs
4 ounces melted butter
1 tablespoon olive oil
1 Spanish onion – diced 1/4 inch
1 green bell pepper – diced 1/4 inch
1 red bell pepper – diced 1/4 inch
2 cups shittake mushrooms – diced 1/4 inch
1/2 tablespoon kosher salt
1/2 tablespoon ground black pepper
1½ pounds cream cheese – softened
4 eggs
1/2 cup heavy cream
1/2 pound smoked Gouda – diced 1/4 inch
1 pound lobster meat – roughly chopped
3 bunch scallions – diced 1/4 inch

Melt butter for crust. Once melted, add to crumbs and Parmesan. Place all ingredients in mixer and mix well for 5 minutes.

Spray 13 x 18 inch sheet pan with pan spray and mold base of wet crust over bottom of pan. With rubber spatula, spread filling into crust about 3/4 of the way to top. Bake on sheet pan for 25 – 40 minutes at 350° or until toothpick dry. Rotate every 15 minutes.

Serves 20.

Lobster Tarragon Crostini

Carol Williams Catering
La Petite Maison
Osterville, MA
Executive Chef Carol Williams

Ingredients:

1 loaf French bread
8 ounces fresh lobster meat
4 ounces grated sharp cheddar cheese
1 teaspoon dried tarragon
1 teaspoon dried parsley
kosher salt and freshly ground pepper to taste
fresh tarragon for garnish

Slice bread into half-inch pieces, lightly toast, and set aside. Dice lobster meat, mix in bowl with cheese and herbs, season to taste. Lightly mound lobster mixture on bread toasts. Place under broiler until cheese starts to melt. Garnish crostini with small sprig of fresh tarragon and serve.

Serves 15 – 20.

Crispy Oysters with Doug's "Green Goddess" Dressing

The Cape Sea Grille
Harwich Port, MA
Chef/Owner Doug Ramler

For the oysters:

Coating:

3/4 cup cornmeal
1/4 cup all-purpose flour
1/2 teaspoon dried ground rosemary
pinch of cayenne pepper
salt and pepper
20 local oysters, shucked
buttermilk
canola oil for frying
chopped flat-leaf parsley
salt and pepper

For the dressing:

2 ripe Hass avocados, pureed
1/2 cup nonfat, plain yogurt, drained through cheesecloth
2 tablespoons fresh lime juice
dash of Tabasco sauce
salt and pepper to taste

For garnish:

1 ripe avocado, peeled and sliced just before serving jarred banana peppers, sliced into rings, optional lemon vinaigrette, optional

Mix together coating ingredients. Mix together dressing ingredients and set aside, refrigerated. Soak the shucked oysters in buttermilk.

Just before serving, heat to 350 enough oil to submerge oysters in deep pan that can hold all oysters (or fry in batches). When oil is hot, dredge oysters in coating and shake to remove excess. Fry the oysters just until they float and carefully flip over for thirty seconds. Remove with slotted spoon and drain on paper towels. Sprinkle with salt, pepper, and chopped parsley. Keep warm.

To serve: Mound five oysters on each serving plate. Drizzle a few tablespoons of dressing around them and garnish with three slices of avocado and the optional banana pepper rings. If desired, drizzle the avocado with a little lemon vinaigrette.

Serves 4.

Oysters Rockefeller

Coonamessett Inn
Falmouth, MA

Ingredients:

12 shucked local oysters
1 12-ounce package of fresh spinach picked
1 cup heavy cream
1 egg
1 shallot chopped
1 clove garlic chopped
1 small onion diced fine
1/4 pound unsalted butter
2 ounces Anisette or Pernod
1/4 bulb fresh fennel diced fine
4 slices white bread diced
4 ounces shredded Gruyere cheese
salt and pepper to taste
1 pinch nutmeg

Preheat oven to 425 degrees.

In a heavy saucepot, melt the butter and sauté the shallot, onion, garlic and fennel until they become soft and translucent. Add the Pernod or Anisette and cook for 1 minute. Add the heavy cream and cook for an additional minute. Season with the nutmeg, salt and pepper. Add the spinach and cook for approximately 30 seconds. Remove from the heat and add the bread and the egg. Let cool briefly. Spoon the spinach mixture onto each oyster and top with some of the Gruyere. Bake in the oven for about 8 – 10 minutes. Serve in two bowls filled with heated rock salt. Garnish with parsley.

The West Falmouth oyster is delicious and many say rivals the Wellfleet oyster down Cape.

Serves 2.

Baked Brie with Cranberries

Ingredients:

1 round Brie
1 unbaked pie crust
1/4 cup whole cranberry sauce
honey mustard
1½ tablespoons packed dark brown sugar

Spread honey mustard on Brie. Mix cranberry sauce and brown sugar. Place Brie on unbaked piecrust. Spread with cranberry mixture. Wrap dough around cheese and seal. Place on greased pie plate.

Bake 350° for 20 minutes or until crust is lightly browned. Serve with bread of choice and crackers.

Sea Scallop Ravioli

Barley Neck Inn & Lodge
Orleans, MA

Sea scallops are substituted for pasta and pounded into thin paillards, stuffed with wild mushrooms, then finished with champagne beurre blanc.

Ingredients:

12 large sea scallops
3 tablespoons olive oil
1/4 pound julienne of shittake mushrooms
1 tablespoon chopped garlic
2 cups champagne or sparkling wine
1 teaspoon chopped thyme
1/4 cup white wine vinegar
1/2 teaspoon chopped rosemary
3 tablespoons heavy cream
4 shallots, chopped
1/2 pound unsalted butter cut into half-inch cubes
12 chives cut into 5-inch lengths, angle the ends

Filling:

Sauté mushrooms in olive oil with garlic, thyme and rosemary. Cook until crispy and chop finely.

Sea scallops:

Slice each scallop in half through the middle, leaving 24 circles. Place halves on a clean cutting board and cover with plastic wrap. With a poultry hammer, press each circle to a thin paillard, about 2 inches in diameter. Place three paillards equidistant on each (oven proof) appetizer plate, salt and pepper. Place a teaspoon of the filling on each paillard.

Place another paillard on top, insuring that the edges of the scallops are touching (scallop will seal itself). Place in a hot oven; bake at 425° for 8 minutes.

Champagne buerre blanc: (recipe will make more than you need)

Combine champagne, white wine vinegar, and chopped shallots in a saucepan. Cook over high heat to reduce until almost dry. Add touch of cream. Bring to a boil. Reduce heat to low. With a thin wisk, add butter slowly until fully dissolved, strain through a fine sieve. Keep warm.

To finish the plates:

Place hot appetizer plate on top of a doilied service plate. Spoon buerre blanc over each ravioli. Place one chive on top of each ravioli, serve immediately.

Serves 4.

Hazelnut Prawns with Coconut Rum Sauce

New Seabury Resort
Mashpee, MA
Executive Chef Josh Zamira

Ingredients:

4 jumbo shrimp (peeled, deveined, cleaned, leave tail on)
2 cups Ritz Crackers (crushed)
1/2 pound hazelnuts peeled
1¼ cups brown sugar
2 cups heavy cream
1 cup all purpose flour
2 cups vegetable oil

Toast hazelnuts in 350 degree oven until golden brown (4-6 minutes).
Let cool.

In food processor, chop hazelnuts (set 4 ounces aside), then add brown
sugar and Ritz crackers. Set breading aside.

Holding the shrimp by the tail, dredge in flour, then dip into heavy
cream. Next place shrimp in hazelnut breading. Press breading onto
shrimp firmly. (Note: When breading shrimp, try to keep the tail, which
you are holding, dry so as not to have breading stick to the tail.)
Proceed with remaining shrimp.

Coconut Rum Sauce:

8 ounces Coco Lopez Crème of Coconut
1/2 quart heavy cream
2 ounces Malibu Rum
1/2 lime

Heat sauce pan and add the rum **(careful, as the rum should ignite)**.

Add heavy cream before liqueur has burned off. Add creme of coconut, juice from 1/2 lime, and remaining hazelnuts set aside earlier. Reduce sauce until slightly thickened.

In separate saucepan, heat vegetable oil to 300 degrees. Place shrimp in oil and fry until golden to dark brown (4-6 minutes).

Serves 1 – 2.

Cranberry Filled Filo Shells

Adrianne P. Lawson

Ingredients:

1/2 cup whole berry cranberry sauce
1/3 cup softened cream cheese
1/4 cup minced crabmeat
2 tablespoons green onion
15 – 18 small filo shells thawed

Preheat oven to 375 degrees. Beat cranberry sauce with fork until smooth. Mix cream cheese, crabmeat, and onion. Fill each filo shell with about 1 teaspoon of cream cheese mixture and top with 1/2 teaspoon cranberry sauce.

Bake 10 minutes until heated through.

The Popponesset Inn's Lamb Chops

Popponesset Inn
Mashpee, MA
Chef Darryl Laman

Ingredients:

3 cups panko (Japanese-style) bread crumbs
2 teaspoons kosher salt
2 teaspoons onion powder
1 teaspoon garlic powder
1 tablespoon dry thyme
2 teaspoons dry rosemary
1 teaspoon ground black pepper
1 tablespoon chopped fresh parsley
1 cup dijon mustard
1 tablespoon honey
2 racks of lamb (7 bones each)

Spread the crumbs on baking sheet. Toast in 350-degree oven until golden brown. Combine the toasted crumbs with the salt, onion powder, garlic powder, thyme, rosemary, black pepper, and parsley. Raise the oven temperature to 400 degrees.

In separate mixing bowl, combine the mustard and honey. Using a sharp knife, cut each lamb rack into individual chops, following the bones. Coat each chop with the mustard mixture, then dredge in the bread crumb mixture.

Arrange the chops on a baking rack set over a sheet pan that will catch the drips. Bake at 400 degrees for 15 minutes. Remove from the oven and let rest for 15 minutes before serving. Individual chops can be eaten as finger food.

Serves 7 – 8.

Stuffed Quahog Clams

Chatham Bars Inn
Chatham, MA
Executive Chef Hidemasa Yamamoto

Ingredients:

1 dozen fresh quahogs chopped (reserve shells)
1 small onion
1 teaspoon finely chopped garlic
2 cups panko Japanese bread crumbs
4 ounces butter
1/4 cup chopped bacon
2 tablespoons chopped green pepper
2 tablespoons chopped red pepper
1 tablespoon fresh lemon juice
1 tablespoon fresh chopped parsley
1 cup clam juice
1/4 cup white wine
2 tablespoons olive oil

Soak clams in clam juice before chopping, pass juice through sieve and reserve. Sauté garlic, onions, and peppers in olive oil and white wine and slowly reduce until almost all the wine has evaporated. Stir (whisk) in all of the butter, then add bacon and bread crumbs. Remove from heat.

Add chopped parsley and clams. If mix is too dry, slowly add reserved clam juice. Stuff clamshells and bake at 350 until hot (about 10 minutes). Top with fresh-squeezed lemon juice.

Smoked Mackerel Creamed Pate

The Dunbar Tea Shop
Sandwich, MA
Chef/Bakers Teresa Keough, Paula Hegarty

Ingredients:

1 pound smoked mackerel, skinned
1/2 pint milk
1½ ounces butter
4 ounces unsalted butter
juice of 1 lemon
bay leaf
1½ ounces flour
salt and pepper

Flake the mackerel and place in a dish. Sprinkle with a little lemon juice and leave to marinate.

Heat the milk and bay leaf to boiling point and leave to infuse in a warm place for 10 – 15 minutes. Remove bay leaf.

Melt the butter in another pan, stir in flour, then the milk, and cook for 1 minute. Remove from heat.

When cold, puree the sauce together with the mackerel, lemon juice, and unsalted butter. Season to taste with extra lemon juice, salt and pepper. Divide evenly between 6 ramekins.

Serves 6.

Quick Crab Pate

The Dunbar Tea Shop
Sandwich, MA
Chef/Bakers Teresa Keough, Paula Hegarty

Ingredients:

4 ounces cream cheese
lemon juice
a little cream (optional)
8 ounces fresh crab meat
salt and pepper
2 tablespoons fresh chopped dill

Beat cream cheese until soft. Add lemon juice, salt, pepper, crab meat, and dill. Mix well. Add a little cream, if too thick. Adjust seasonings if necessary. Divide evenly between 6 ramekins.

Serves 6.

THE CAPE COD CHRISTMAS COOKBOOK

Mushroom and Walnut Pate

The Dunbar Tea Shop
Sandwich, MA
Chef/Bakers Teresa Keough, Paula Hegarty

Ingredients:

6 ounces mushrooms
2 tablespoons sunflower oil
1 large garlic, crushed
1/4 teaspoon salt
freshly grated nutmeg
fresh chopped herbs of your choice
6 ounces cream cheese
juice of 1/2 lemon
1½ ounces chopped walnuts
dash of Tabasco
salt and pepper

Wash, peel, slice the mushrooms. Save 4 smallish pieces to garnish. Heat 1½ tablespoons of oil and sauté the mushrooms for 2 minutes. Remove mushrooms from pan with a slotted spoon. Place in liquidizer with the cheese, garlic and lemon juice. Mix together, then season with Tabasco, nutmeg, salt and pepper to taste.

Add the remaining oil to pan with the juice from the mushrooms and cook the walnuts with a sprinkling of salt for 3 – 4 minutes. When cool, fold the nuts into the blended cheese/mushroom mixture.

Divide between 4 ramekins; decorate with mushroom slices and herbs. Chill until ready to serve.

Serves 4.

Hanukkah Harry's Potato Pancakes

Ingredients:

4 medium potatoes, peeled
2 eggs
1 teaspoon salt
1/2 cup flour
1/2 teaspoon baking powder
1 teaspoon onion

Put potatoes in food processor with onion. Strain excess water. Add other ingredients, stirring well. Drop batter by tablespoon into 1/8 inch of hot vegetable oil. Fry on both sides until golden brown. Serve with sour cream or applesauce.

Herring with Cranberries

Ingredients:

1 large jar herring tidbits
1/2 pint sour cream
1/2 can whole cranberry sauce
1 medium red onion sliced very thin

Drain herring well and remove onions. Mix remaining ingredients with herring. Place in refrigerator until cold. Serve with cocktail rye bread.

Note: More cranberry sauce can be used if you want a sweeter dip.

Chopped Herring

Ingredients:

1 large jar herring tidbits, drained
1 small apple, peeled
2 slices of egg bread (white bread can be used) soaked in juice
    from jar of herring
1/2 small onion (more can be used)
3 hard-boiled eggs
1 teaspoon sugar (or to taste)

Put all of the above ingredients except one of the hard-boiled eggs into a chopping bowl. Chop very fine. Ingredients can also be put through a grinder. Mix thoroughly and put into a serving bowl. Use yolk from reserved hard-boiled egg and put through a strainer, garnish on top of herring. Serve with crackers or cocktail rye bread.

Captain Irving Gardner's Fish Chowder

Captain Gardner grew up in Harwich Port and later became a Boston Harbor pilot. A cook on one of the original schooner pilot boats taught him how to make the real New England fish chowder.

Ingredients:

4 pounds haddock fillets, skinned
1 backbone of haddock
1 pound halibut steak, skinned, bone in
3 large potatoes, sliced 1/4 inch thick (half dollar size)
1 large onion, diced
1/2 pound salt pork, diced 1/2 inch
1 quart milk
1 pint light cream
1 teaspoon sugar
salt and pepper to taste
1/2 pound butter

Cut haddock and backbone into large pieces. Place in heavy kettle with whole halibut steak. Just cover with water and add sugar. Cook on low heat (do not boil) until fish is firm. Do not overcook. In separate kettle, warm milk, cream, butter, salt and pepper.

Fry pork scraps in large frying pan. When scraps are brown, remove from oil and drain on paper towels. Reduce heat to low and add diced onions. Cook until just tender. Add potatoes and water. Cover and bring to a boil. Cook until potatoes are done. Add to warming milk. If potatoes are cooked separately, as in a large chowder, some of the potato water should be added to the milk.

Remove bones from the cooked fish. Add fish to warming milk, being careful to keep fish in large chunks. Use fish water to thin chowder as desired. Salt to taste. Put a few pork scraps in each bowl of chowder.

Serves 8 – 10.

Asparagus Bisque with Creme Fraiche and Smoked Salmon

The Cape Sea Grille
Harwich Port, MA
Chef/Owner Doug Ramler

"This is a favorite soup of CSG when there are still cool nights around Cape Cod, but the early touches of spring have begun to offer us some local produce." – Doug

Ingredients:

1 pound asparagus, bottom ends discarded
2 ½ quarts chicken stock or vegetable stock
1 medium sized yellow onion, roughly chopped
2 leeks, chopped, washed
2 cloves garlic, peeled, chopped
2 tablespoons fresh thyme, picked, chopped
2 tablespoons fresh tarragon, picked, chopped
1 cup white wine
4 large Idaho potatoes, peeled, medium dice

Optional:

heavy cream, to taste
creme fraiche, to taste
smoked salmon, sliced thin, to garnish

Cut enough tips off the asparagus for garnish and reserve for later.

Heat a large stockpot and add a small amount of oil, the onions, leeks, garlic, and fresh herbs. Allow the ingredients to soften but do not brown. Add the potatoes, wine, and stock. Bring the liquid to a boil and turn down to a simmer.

As the liquid is heating, shred the asparagus in a food processor. Place the asparagus tips in a strainer and blanch them in the hot liquid until tender. Cool them immediately and reserve for serving.

Simmer the liquid until the potatoes are just soft. Add the shredded asparagus and continue cooking until asparagus is just tender. Remove from heat and puree the entire mixture with a blender or in batches with the processor. Pass the pureed mixture through a fine strainer that will catch all of the shredded asparagus. Make sure to press the mixture hard to extract all the flavor.

Season with salt and pepper and chill immediately, uncovered, if not serving.

Optional steps:

Reheat and add equal parts of cream to desired taste. Check seasoning. Garnish each bowl with a few asparagus tips and a little smoked salmon.

Serves 12.

Butternut Bisque

Impudent Oyster
Chatham, MA
Executive Chef Lou Concra

Ingredients:

5 pounds diced butternut squash
1 quart + 1 cup vegetable stock

Cook squash in stock until tender, puree and return to medium heat.

Add:

1 pint heavy cream
3 cups light cream
1 ounce vegetable bouillon
3/4 cup real maple syrup
1/2 teaspoon white pepper

Heat slowly, stirring frequently until thick.

Ginger-Carrot Bisque

Chatham Squire Restaurant
Chatham, MA
Executive Chef Robert Davis

Ingredients:

8 ounces fresh ginger, chopped
1 pound potatoes, peeled & diced
1 large onion, diced
1 tablespoon garlic, minced
2 pounds carrots, rough chop
4 ounces butter
2 46-ounce cans chicken broth
1 quart heavy cream
4 ounces cream sherry
1 tablespoon ground ginger
1 cup brown sugar
1 tablespoon dry oregano
salt and pepper to taste

In a heavy-bottomed pot, add the butter, fresh ginger, potatoes, onions, garlic, and carrots. Sweat over medium heat until onions are translucent. Add chicken broth, brown sugar, oregano, and ground ginger. Bring to a boil and cook until vegetables are tender.

Puree mixture in batches using a blender or food processor. Return puree to pot and add the sherry (puree should be somewhat thick). Add the heavy cream to the desired consistency. Add salt & pepper to taste. Cook over low heat for 30 minutes.

Tip: If soup is too thin, you may thicken it with instant potatoes.

German Apple and Onion Bisque

Bramble Inn & Restaurant
Brewster, MA
Chef/Owner Ruth Manchester

"This easy and creamy soup takes advantage of items you usually already have on hand. If you don't have a fruity wine, use any white wine and adjust with a little sugar." – Ruth

Ingredients:

1 stick butter
1 Spanish onion chopped fine
2 large carrots scraped and chopped fine
3 Granny Smith apples cored and chopped fine
1 tablespoon caraway seeds
1½ cups Moselle or any light fruity slightly sweet wine
4 cups chicken stock
8 ounces softened cream cheese
1/2 teaspoon salt
1/4 teaspoon white pepper

Sauté vegetables and apple in butter until soft. Add seasonings, wine, and stock and cook, stirring occasionally for about 20 minutes. Strain out 1/2 cup vegetable-apple mixture and reserve. In blender in batches, puree soup with chunks of cream cheese until smooth. Add reserved vegetable-apple mixture and heat back up. Adjust seasoning and add more stock if too thick.

Serves 8 – 10.

Snowy Day Chicken Soup

A wonderful soup to warm you up on a cold day!

Ingredients:

2-3 pounds chicken
4 carrots, peeled
2 parsnips, peeled
1 large onion
salt and pepper to taste

Place chicken in large pot. Add water to cover chicken (about 2 inches over the chicken). Add remaining ingredients. Bring to a boil. Reduce heat and simmer until chicken is tender — 2½ hours. Cover while simmering. Skim top during cooking to make sure soup is clear.

Serves 6.

Holiday Cabbage Soup with Gingersnaps

Michael Jasper

My father has been making this delicious soup for years.

Ingredients:

1 large can sauerkraut
2 large cans of tomatoes
3 pounds of your favorite soup meat
1/2 cup brown sugar
6 gingersnaps (crushed)

Put all ingredients in pot with water to cover. Bring to a boil, reduce heat and simmer for approximately 2 hours until meat is tender. The longer the soup stands the better it is.

THE CAPE COD CHRISTMAS COOKBOOK

Main Courses and Side Dishes

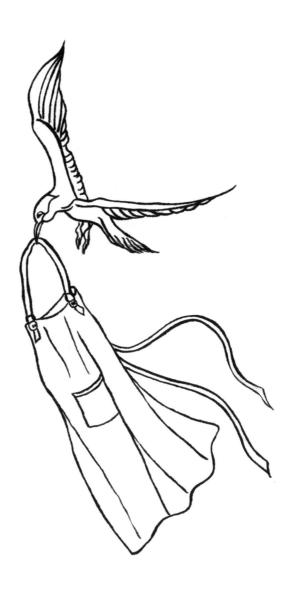

Haddock De Journee

The Colonial House Inn
Yarmouth Port, MA
Executive Chef Ivan Velinov

Ingredients:

2 pounds haddock, fillet
4 ounces shrimp, chopped fine
4 ounces scallops, chopped fine
2 ounces lobster, chopped fine
pinch of salt and pepper
1/2 ounce (1 tablespoon) lemon juice
1 ounce (2 tablespoons) white wine
1 tablespoon Worcestershire sauce
pinch of thyme
1/2 cup heavy cream

Combine all ingredients except haddock and heavy cream in a stainless steel mixing bowl. Place bowl over ice. Add cream slowly, whipping constantly with a wire whisk until mixture is well blended. Butter an ovenproof baking dish. Slit haddock to make a pocket, and stuff with mixture. Place in dish and bake at 350 for 20 minutes or until fish flakes when tested. Before serving top with Hollandaise sauce.

Hollandaise Sauce — Makes 1 cup

1/2 cup melted, warm butter
4 tablespoons boiling water
1 1/2 tablespoons lemon juice or tarragon vinegar
1/4 teaspoon salt
pinch of cayenne
3 egg yolks

Place egg yolks in double boiler (cook over hot water — NOT boiling water), stirring constantly with wire whisk until they begin to thicken. Add 1 tablespoon boiling water. Repeat until all 4 tablespoons of water have been added. Beat in warm lemon juice. Remove from heat. Add warm melted butter very slowly, beating constantly with wire whisk. Add salt and cayenne. Serve at once.

HINT: Can be stored in large-mouth thermos jar until serving time.

Serves 4 to 6.

Cape Cod Christmas Scallops

The Bee-Hive Tavern
Sandwich, MA

"Christmas time on Cape Cod is also the time of year that those incredibly delicious little Nantucket Bay scallops are in season. Fresh sea scallops will also work but the 'Bays' are available. They're worth the premium you'll pay." – Bob King (Proprietor)

Ingredients:

3 pounds Nantucket Bay scallops
1 tablespoon olive oil
2 navel oranges
1/2 cup dried cranberries (more if you desire)
fresh chopped parsley for garnish

Preheat oven to 450 degrees. Toss scallops and dried cranberries in a bowl with olive oil until coated. Place in 9-inch baking dish and squeeze the juice from 2 navel oranges over the scallops and bake for 10 minutes. Remove from oven and sprinkle with fresh chopped parsley.

Serves 6.

Beef Tenderloin with Cranberries

Janet Kelsey

Ingredients:

1 3-pound beef tenderloin
1 cup dried cranberries
1 cup cranberry juice
1 cup tawny port wine
3 tablespoons brown sugar
2 tablespoons soy sauce
1 teaspoon pepper
3 cloves garlic, minced
1 tablespoon flour

Combine tenderloin and next 7 ingredients in a large plastic bag, seal bag and marinate in refrigerator 24 hours turning bag occasionally. Remove tenderloin from bag, reserving marinade. Preheat oven to 500 degrees. Put tenderloin in a broiler pan coated with cooking spray. Place in oven and immediately reduce oven to 350 degrees. Bake one hour and 10 minutes or until thermometer reaches 145 – 160 degrees (depending on how you like the meat cooked). Let stand 15 minutes before slicing.

Combine flour and 2 tablespoons of reserved marinade in a saucepan, stir with whisk. Add remaining marinade to saucepan, stir until blended. Bring to a boil, reduce heat and cook 8 minutes or until thick, stirring constantly. Serve warm with tenderloin.

Serves 5 – 6.

Tournedos of Beef Powerscourt with Grilled Shrimp, Asparagus and Mashed Potatoes

Coonamessett Inn
Falmouth, MA

Beef Ingredients:

4 4-ounce beef tenderloin steaks
4 jumbo shrimp, peeled, deveined and marinated in lemon juice, olive oil, salt and pepper
1 shallot, chopped
1 large tomato, peeled, seeded and diced
2 ounces Irish Whiskey
4 ounces heavy cream
1 pinch cracked black pepper
1 pinch coarsely chopped parsley
12 asparagus spears, trimmed and blanched
salt and pepper
2 ounces olive oil

Beef instructions:

Heat a heavy sauté pan and add the olive oil. Season the tournedos with salt and pepper. Place the tournedos in the sauté pan. Brown on both sides, remove from pan and reserve. Sauté shallot, add the whiskey and reduce by one-half. Add the cream and cook until it becomes a sauce consistency. Add the tomatoes, black pepper and parsley. Heat the asparagus in butter, salt and pepper. Put the shrimp on the grill, one minute per side. Put the tournedos on the plate first, then sauce the beef and put one grilled shrimp on top of each tournedos. Pipe the potatoes on each plate and finish with the asparagus spears.

Mashed Potato Ingredients:

4 medium-sized Yukon gold potatoes
2 ounces butter
2 ounces heavy cream
salt and pepper to taste

Mashed potato instructions:

Peel the potatoes, put in pot and cover with cold salted water. Bring to a boil and cook thoroughly. Drain, add butter, and mash. Add cream and check seasoning. Put into a pastry bag with a large star tip.

Serves 2.

Grilled Tuna Steak
with Tomato-Caper Chutney

Lobster Pot
Provincetown, MA
Chef/Owner Tim McNulty

Ingredients:

2 10-ounce tuna steaks
daikon radish, shredded

Marinade (1 quart):

16 ounces peanut oil
8 ounces soy sauce
1 tablespoon honey
1 tablespoon dijon mustard
1/2 pound onion, pureed
1 tablespoon ginger root, pureed
1 tablespoon garlic, pureed

(Note: this marinade can be used several times before being discarded.)

Chutney:

1 large tomato, seeded and chopped
4 ounces cucumber, seeded, peeled and diced
1 teaspoon capers, drained and rinsed
1 tablespoon scallions, sliced thin
1/2 teaspoon ginger root pureed
1/2 teaspoon garlic, pureed
pinch black pepper

<u>To make the marinade:</u> Place all ingredients in a bowl and blend with a wire whisk, or put them in a food processor. (This can be made 4 days ahead of time.)

<u>To make the chutney:</u> Place all ingredients in a sauté pan and cook slowly for about 15 minutes. Mix until blended well. (This can be made 2 days ahead of time.)

Marinate tuna for 10 minutes. Shake off excess marinade and grill for about 4 minutes on each side, depending upon thickness of steaks. Serve with raw daikon radish and warm chutney.

Serves 2.

Christmas Cod

Simple and delicious!

Ingredients:

1 pound codfish fillet
1/2 sleeve Ritz Crackers, crushed
4-5 tablespoons butter, melted
1/4 cup pecans, crushed
1 tablespoon fresh chopped parsley
fresh lemon juice
olive oil

Drizzle lemon juice and olive oil over fish. Combine Ritz Crackers, melted butter, parsley, and pecans together. Spread crumb mixture evenly over fillets. Bake in 350 degree oven for approximately 20 – 22 minutes, depending upon thickness.

Serves 2.

Christmas Cranberry Chicken

Ingredients:

6 large split chicken breasts with bones
1 can (16 ounces) whole cranberry sauce
1 package dry onion soup mix
1 bottle of Lite French dressing (8 ounces)
1/3 cup orange juice
Sweet and hot mustard

Spread mustard lightly over chicken breasts. Place in 13 x 9 inch glass baking dish. Mix cranberry sauce, onion soup mix, French dressing, and orange juice. Pour over chicken. Bake at 350 1 hour and 15 minutes or until done.

Serves 6.

Chicken and Butternut Ravioli

Yarmouth House Restaurant
Yarmouth, MA
Executive Chef Gary Sprague

Ingredients:

4 boneless chicken breasts, cleaned and slightly pounded
1 cup carrots julienned
1 cup turnips, julienned
12 butternut-stuffed ravioli
1/2 teaspoon minced shallot
1/2 teaspoon minced garlic
2 ounces dried cranberries
3 ounces Madeira wine
6 ounces chicken gravy
4 ounces heavy cream
2 ounces unsalted butter

In salted water cook carrots and turnips until almost tender. Then cool in a bath of ice water. Do the same with ravioli. Then drain both and set aside.

Season chicken breasts with salt and pepper. Dredge in flour and place in hot skillet containing 2 ounces oil. Brown on both sides, then discard any excess oil. Add garlic, shallot, and Madeira wine to pan. Reduce wine by half. Add gravy, cream, turnip, carrots, cranberries, and ravioli. Reduce heat to simmer and cook until sauce thickens. Just before serving, wisk in unsalted butter, garnish with toasted almonds if desired.

Butternut ravioli are available in most specialty pasta stores or can be made at home using wonton wrappers or pasta sheets and a filling of 3 parts cooked squash to one part ricotta cheese, seasoned with salt, pepper, nutmeg, and cinnamon to taste.

Serves 4.

Sea of Love

Christian's Restaurant
Chatham, MA
Executive Chef Don Dickerson

Ingredients:

2 ounces olive oil
3 medium-sized shrimp – peeled and deveined (tail off)
2 ounces scallops – picked and washed
2 ounces sliced mushrooms
3 artichoke hearts – quartered
1 ounce minced garlic
1 ounce minced shallots
1 ounce sundried tomatoes – chopped fine
2 ounces plum tomatoes – diced
3 scallions – green only, rough chop
2 leaves basil – chiffonade
2 ounces fresh lobster meat
2 ounces white wine (Chablis is nice)
2 ounces beurre blanc (any butter sauce will work)
salt and pepper to taste
1 ounce shredded Parmesan
1 teaspoon parsley – chopped fine
4 ounces cooked penne pasta

In skillet add olive oil and drop shrimp and scallops. Once hot, add white wine and flip seafood. Add all veggies and sauté until well distributed. Add lobster meat and beurre blanc and toss well. Season with salt/pepper and toss with penne pasta. Garnish with shredded Parmesan and chopped parsley. Serve hot!

Serves 1.

Pan Seared Saffron Scallops Choron

Sea Crest Oceanfront Resort
North Falmouth, MA
Executive Chef Lee H. Ei

Ingredients:

1 pound fresh scallops
1 large ripe tomato (peeled, seeded and chopped)
1 tablespoon chopped shallots
1 cup white wine
2 tablespoons olive oil
3 tablespoons whole butter
1/4 cup heavy cream
1 pinch saffron
salt and pepper to taste
1 pound cooked white rice

Heat olive oil in medium sauté pan. Sear off scallops until golden brown. Add chopped tomatoes, shallots – sauté until hot. Add white wine and saffron and allow to reduce by 2/3rds. Add heavy cream and reduce by half. Swirl in whole butter and serve over a bed of white rice. Garish with parsley or chopped fresh chives.

Serves 2 – 3.

Salmon Homard

Sea Crest Oceanfront Resort
North Falmouth, MA
Executive Chef Lee H. Ei

Ingredients:

2 6-ounce salmon fillets
4 ounces chopped lobster meat
2 ounces olive oil
1 cup seasoned flour
1 cup eggs, beaten
1/2 cup white wine
1 ounce lemon juice
2 ounces whole butter
chopped parsley
salt and pepper to taste

Dredge salmon fillets in flour. Dip in egg. Heat oil in sauté pan –
medium heat. Place egg-dipped salmon skin side up. Sauté until golden
brown. Turn over salmon and brown other side. Add white wine and
cook salmon on low heat until cooked, about 5 – 8 minutes. Add lobster
meat, lemon juice, and whole butter. Salt and pepper to taste. Garnish
with chopped parsley.

Serves 2.

Salmon Pistache

Barley Neck Inn & Lodge
Orleans, MA

Ingredients for the salmon:

Tarragon Chablis sauce (recipe follows)
1 pound salmon filet, skinned and boned, halved
1/4 cup peeled pistachio nuts
1/4 cup toasted pine nuts
2 tablespoons oil
salt and pepper to taste

Prepare the sauce and keep warm. Preheat the oven to 350. Chop the two nuts together finely. Heat the oil in a sauté pan that can be placed in the oven over medium-high heat. When hot, sauté the salmon on both sides, about 2 minutes each side. Remove from heat, salt and pepper, and coat with the pistachio/pine nut mixture. Place pan in oven and cook fish through, about 4 minutes.

To serve: Spoon the white wine sauce over the salmon.

Tarragon Chablis Sauce:

1/3 cup dry white wine, such as Chablis
1 shallot, finely chopped
2 teaspoons fresh tarragon, finely chopped
1 plum tomato, seeded and diced
1/2 cup heavy cream
salt/pepper to taste

Add the shallot to the white wine and reduce over medium-low heat in a small pan until almost dry. Add the cream, tarragon, and diced tomatoes. At the last minute, add salt and pepper to taste. Set aside and keep warm.

Serves 2.

Salmon and Tarragon Twist

The Dunbar Tea Shop
Sandwich, MA
Chef/Bakers Teresa Keough, Paula Hegarty

Ingredients:

3 pounds side of fresh salmon, skin and bones removed
juice and rind of 1 lemon
4 tablespoons fresh parsley
2 tablespoons fresh tarragon
salt and pepper
1 sheet puff pastry

Cut side of salmon in half crossways. Sprinkle bigger piece with salt, pepper, lemon rind, and juice. Spread herbs thickly over. Put other half on top, skin side up.

Roll out pastry into rectangle twice the width of, and slightly longer than, the salmon. Dust lightly with flour and fold width-wise in half. Cut diagonally down edge going about halfway towards the crease. Open pastry out again.

Place salmon in middle of pastry and taking alternate strips, fold the pastry over the salmon so that the strips of pastry overlap one another in the middle to form a plait. Brush the pastry well with beaten egg and bake at 350 until golden brown (about 45 minutes). This dish can be eaten hot (delicious with Hollandaise Sauce) or cold.

Serves 6.

Cornish Pasty

The Dunbar Tea Shop
Sandwich, MA
Chef/Bakers Teresa Keough, Paula Hegarty

Ingredients:

5 pounds ground beef
2 large onions, chopped
5 potatoes, diced and peeled
3 tablespoons Worcestershire sauce
2 eggs, beaten
3 large carrots, diced
4 garlic cloves, crushed
salt and pepper
puff pastry squares 6 x 6 inches

Brown the ground beef, onions, and garlic in large sauté pan. In separate pan boil potatoes and carrots until soft. Mix together the beef and potatoes and carrots, add Worcestershire sauce, salt and pepper to taste. Cool slightly.

Roll out the puff pastry squares to 8 x 8 inches. Place 1/2 to 3/4 cup filling in middle of pastry. Brush edges with egg. Draw up from opposite diagonal sides to meet on top of mound. Crimp edges to seal. Brush with beaten egg and sprinkle with mixed herbs. Pierce with fork. Bake in 400 oven for 20 – 25 minutes until golden brown. Top with beef gravy.

Serves 24.

Steak and Kidney Pie

The Dunbar Tea Shop
Sandwich, MA
Chef/Bakers Teresa Keough, Paula Hegarty

Ingredients:

1 sheet puff pastry or shortcrust pastry
salt and pepper
6 ounces kidney, skinned and cored
1/4 pint beef stock
2 teaspoons mixed herbs
1 egg beaten with milk
2 tablespoons flour
1½ pounds braising steak, cubed
1 large onion, chopped
1/4 pint beer
1 tablespoon Worcestershire sauce
1 ounce butter

Preheat oven to 400. Season 1 ounce of flour with salt and pepper, then toss the steak and chopped kidney in the flour.

Melt 1 ounce of butter in a large saucepan and fry the onion until soft, about 5 minutes. Add the steak and kidney with remaining flour and cook for 5 minutes until lightly browned. Gradually stir in stock, beer, herbs, and Worcestershire sauce. Cover and simmer gently for 1¼ hours. Spoon mixture into a 9-inch pie plate. Top with pastry and crimp the edges, garnish with pastry leaves, brush with egg. Bake for 35 – 45 minutes until golden.

Serves 6 – 8.

Winter Goulash

A hearty dish, best served on a cold winter's day.

Ingredients:

1 pound steak (sirloin strip) thinly sliced
1 teaspoon oil
1 onion chopped
2 cloves garlic minced
1 28-ounce can crushed tomatoes, undrained
1/2 cup water
1/2 cup red wine (optional)
1½ tablespoons paprika
1 teaspoon salt
1/2 teaspoon pepper
6-8 ounces broad noodles (cooked 3 – 4 minutes and drained)
1 cup sour cream
2 tablespoons flour

Cook half the meat in frying pan until brown. Remove from pan. Cook remaining meat with garlic and onion until meat is brown and onions are soft and golden. Drain fat from pan. Add all the meat, undrained can of tomatoes, water, paprika, salt and pepper in large saucepan. Cook until a light boil. Add noodles, stir – reduce heat and cook about 15 minutes. Stir flour into sour cream and add to mixture. Cook until bubbly and thick.

You can use chicken instead of meat.

Serves 4 – 6.

Clam Pie

Grace Nyberg

One of the most famous clam pie recipes on Cape Cod.

Ingredients:

Pastry for a 2 crust 9-inch pie
3 cups raw ground quahog or sea clams
1/2 cup finely chopped onion
1 cup fine cracker crumbs (Pilot crackers are best)
1/2 cup evaporated milk
1/4 teaspoon freshly ground pepper
1/4 teaspoon dried thyme

Line a 9-inch pie plate with pastry. Mix clams, onions, and crumbs with milk and seasonings. Spoon into pie shell. Cover with pastry and seal edges. Cut several slits in top. Bake at 425 for about 50 minutes or until nicely browned.

Serves 4 – 6.

Bacalhao a Braz

A fantastic Portuguese recipe!
Perfect for your Cape Cod holiday table.

1 large onion (chopped)
2 tablespoons hot red crushed pepper
5 tablespoons olive oil
1/2 bar butter
1 teaspoon paprika
2-4 cloves garlic
6-8 medium potatoes (cubed)
parsley
1 pound salted codfish

Soak cod sufficiently to remove excess salt. Cook and let cool and then shred. Deep-fry potatoes. Sauté the above ingredients. Mix codfish in sautéed mixture. Keep heat low and cook for approximately 5 minutes. After potatoes are done, mix in with codfish. Beat 2 eggs and mix in with cod and potatoes. Cod should have a reddish appearance. Add salt if needed, and sprinkle with parsley on top if desired.

Serves 2.

Butternut Squash Casserole

Ingredients for squash:

3 cups peeled butternut squash
1/4 cup butter
2 tablespoons brown sugar
1/4 teaspoon salt
dash of white pepper

Boil or steam squash 20 – 30 minutes, mash. Add butter to mashed squash. Add brown sugar and salt/pepper. Mix until butter is melted.

Ingredients for apples:

6 cups sliced and peeled apples (skin can be left on)
2 teaspoons butter
1/4 cup sugar

Ingredients for topping:

1½ cups crushed cornflakes
1/2 cup chopped pecans
1/2 cup brown sugar
2 tablespoons melted butter

Heat 2 teaspoons butter in skillet, add sliced apples, sprinkle with 1/4 cup sugar, cover and simmer over low heat, about 4 – 5 minutes. Spread apples in casserole dish, spoon squash over apples. Mix topping ingredients and sprinkle topping over casserole. Bake 15 minutes at 350 degrees.

Serves 4 – 6.

Carrot Soufflé

Janet Kelsey

Ingredients:

2 cups cooked carrots, mashed
2 teaspoons lemon juice
2 tablespoons minced onion
1/2 cup butter, softened
1/4 cup sugar
1 tablespoon flour
1 teaspoon salt
1/4 teaspoon cinnamon
1 cup whole milk
3 eggs

In an electric mixer put hot carrots and butter. Mix on low speed until butter is melted and carrots are mashed. Add remaining ingredients and blend well. Pour into well-greased casserole dish. Bake 50 – 60 minutes at 350 degrees uncovered until hot.

Serves 6.

Apple Noodle Pudding

One of my favorite side dishes.

Ingredients:

2 apples (peeled, cored and chopped)
1 pound wide noodles
1/4 pound melted butter
1 pint sour cream
4 eggs
1 pound cottage cheese
4 tablespoons sugar
1/4 teaspoon salt
1 glass milk
1 teaspoon vanilla
1/2 cup cornflake crumbs
1/4 cup brown sugar

Cook noodles about 5 to 6 minutes. Drain and combine noodles, butter, sour cream and 2 eggs plus cottage cheese, sugar, apples, salt, and vanilla. Mix well. Spread in 13 x 9 inch greased pan. Mix 2 eggs beaten with a glass of milk. Pour over noodle mixture. Mix 1/2 cup cornflake crumbs with 1/4 cup brown sugar. Sprinkle over top. Bake 50 minutes at 350°. Let set 10 minutes before slicing. Serve with sour cream.

Serves 12.

Colonial Corn Pudding

Ingredients:

1 can creamed corn
1 cup milk
2 tablespoons flour
2 eggs, beaten
1 tablespoon melted butter
2 tablespoons sugar

Mix ingredients together. Bake in 350 degree oven for 50 – 60 minutes or until golden brown.

Serves 4.

Sweet Glazed Turnips and Carrots

Sheila and Peter Allard

2 large rutabaga turnips
1 large bag of carrots
1 cup brown sugar (tightly packed)
1 stick of butter
salt and pepper to taste

Peel carrots and turnips. Cut both vegetables into bite-size pieces. Boil in a large pot of water until they are slightly soft. Drain water, then put vegetables back into pot. Add brown sugar, butter, salt and pepper. Cover pan and shake to mix together (if you use a spoon to mix mixture you will crush the vegetables).

Serves 6 – 8.

Cranberry Relish Mold

Ingredients:

1 cup boiling water
2 packages raspberry gelatin
1½ cups cold water
1/2 cup mandarin oranges, drained
1 8-ounce can pineapple tidbits, drained
1 can whole cranberry sauce
1/2 cup chopped nuts (optional)

Dissolve gelatin in hot water. Add cold water and mix, then add the cranberry sauce. Line mold with mandarin oranges, cover with pineapple and nuts. Pour gelatin mixture over all and chill until firm.

Christmas Cranberry Sauce

Ingredients:

1/2 cup sugar
1/2 cup brown sugar, packed
2 cups cranberries

Combine the sugars and one cup of water in a saucepan. Bring to a boil, stirring until the sugar is dissolved. Boil for 5 minutes over medium heat, stirring often. Add the cranberries and reduce heat. Boil slowly about 4 minutes. Stir occasionally. Cool mixture before serving.

Note: A small amount of cinnamon can be added for a spicy flavor.

Mom's Old-Fashioned Stuffing

Marilyn Jasper

Ingredients:

1 16-ounce loaf egg bread
1 16-ounce corn bread
2 large carrots
3 large onions, sautéed until golden brown
1 sleeve Ritz Crackers
2 eggs
2 peeled potatoes
1/2 to 3/4 cup dried cranberries
chicken broth (about 22 ounces)
salt and pepper to taste

In food processor, put the carrots, potatoes, crackers, and eggs. Blend until carrots and potatoes are chopped fine. Pour into large bowl. Add the sautéed onions, corn bread, and egg bread. Pour the chicken broth over all until mixture is no longer dry. Mixture should be very moist. Add salt and pepper and dried cranberries. Mix well, pour into well greased large casserole dish. Bake at 350 degrees for about 1 hour to 1 hour and 20 minutes.

Serves 12.

Desserts

Cranberry Pie

Ashley Manor Bed & Breakfast
Barnstable, MA

Ingredients:

2 cups fresh or frozen cranberries
1 cup fresh or frozen blueberries
1/2 cup nuts
1/4 cup melted butter
1 cup flour
1 cup sugar
2 beaten eggs
1/2 cup melted butter
1 teaspoon vanilla extract

Line 9 inch pie plate with fresh or frozen berries. Sprinkle with the nuts and the 1/4 cup of melted butter. Combine the remaining ingredients, mix well and pour over the berry mixture. Bake at 325 degrees for 35 – 40 minutes

Serves 8.

Cranberry Bread Pudding

Coonamessett Inn
Falmouth, MA

Ingredients:

1 loaf day-old bread cut into cubes
4 eggs
2 cups heavy cream
1 cup sugar
2 ounces brandy
2 cups dried cranberries
1 tablespoon cinnamon

Blend eggs, cream, sugar, cinnamon, brandy, and cranberries. Add bread to mixture and let stand for 2 – 4 hours.

Heat oven to 350 degrees. Butter a baking dish and add bread mixture to it. Place dish in a water bath and cover with aluminum foil and bake for 45 minutes. Remove foil and bake for an additional 15 minutes. Remove from the water bath and cool.

Serve with a dusting of powdered sugar and sweetened whipped cream.

Serves 8.

Apple Cranberry Bread Pudding

Chatham Bar's Inn
Chatham, MA
Executive Chef Hidemasa Yamamoto

Ingredients:

Caramel Sauce:

1 cup water
1½ cups sugar
1 cup heavy cream
2 ounces butter

Cook water and sugar until caramel turns a medium amber. Slowly whisk in heavy cream. Add butter. Whisk until combined. Chill over ice bath.

Bread Pudding:

3 Granny Smith apples
1 1/2 cups fresh cranberries
2 ounces butter
1/4 cup sugar
6 eggs
4 egg yolks
1½ cups heavy cream
1½ cups light cream or half-and-half
2 teaspoons vanilla extract
1 cup sugar
1 cup caramel sauce (see above recipe)
1 teaspoon cinnamon
1/2 teaspoon nutmeg
1/2 teaspoon ginger
1 pound cubed croissants or bread

Peel, core, and slice apples. Heat butter. Add sliced apples and cranberries. Add 1/4 cup sugar. Sauté until cooked, about 10 minutes. Chill.

Whisk together eggs, egg yolks, heavy cream, light cream, vanilla, sugar, caramel sauce, cinnamon, nutmeg, and ginger. Add cubed croissants or bread. Combine. Add cooled apples and cranberries. Spread into greased 9 x 9 inch pan. Bake in water bath until set and golden brown (about 50 minutes). Serve warm with ice cream or sweetened whipped cream.

Serves 12.

White Christmas Pumpkin Cheesecake

Marilyn Jasper

A rich and creamy cheesecake that ages like a fine red wine. The longer it stands the more delicious it becomes.

Crust:

1 cup vanilla wafers, crushed fine
1/2 cup gingersnaps, crushed fine
4 tablespoons melted butter

Pie:

24 ounces softened cream cheese
1 cup + 3 tablespoons sugar
2 eggs
1 1/2 teaspoons cinnamon
1/2 teaspoon nutmeg
1/2 teaspoon ginger
1 15-ounce can pumpkin
3/4 cup light cream
2 tablespoons cornstarch
2 teaspoons vanilla

Topping:

1 1/2 cups sour cream
1/3 cup packed brown sugar
1 teaspoon vanilla

Combine crushed cookie crumbs with melted butter. Spread into 9-inch greased springform pan.

In electric mixer, beat cream cheese, add sugar, beat about 2 minutes. Add eggs, pumpkin, blend well. Add the vanilla, cinnamon, ginger, and nutmeg. Continue beating and slowly add cream and then the cornstarch. Beat until all is blended and smooth (about 5 minutes). Pour into crust. Bake at 350 degrees about 50 – 55 minutes until center moves slightly.

Topping:

Combine sour cream, vanilla, and brown sugar. Mix well. Take cheesecake out of oven and carefully spread topping over top. Put back in oven for 5 minutes. Cool at least 40 minutes before refrigerating. When cool, run knife along sides of springform to loosen.

Serves 10.

Ruth's Bramble Inn Flourless Chocolate Cake

Bramble Inn & Restaurant
Brewster, MA
Chef/Owner Ruth Manchester

"We have been serving this rich moist cake at the inn long before 'flourless' became so popular. It is so easy to make and clean up after, and it gets rave reviews every time." – Ruth

Ingredients:

12 ounces good quality semi-sweet chocolate
1 cup sugar
1/2 cup water
4 large eggs
1 stick unsalted butter, softened and cut into 6 pieces

Break chocolate into small pieces. Place in work bowl of food processor and process to a fine grind. Combine sugar and water together in small saucepan. Bring to boil and boil hard 3 minutes. With processor on, pour hot sugar syrup down feed tube and process until chocolate is melted. Add butter in pieces and process until all incorporated. Add eggs, one at a time and process smooth.

Spray sides and bottom of a 9-inch cake tin with vegetable oil spray. Line bottom with round of wax paper and spray again. Pour batter evenly into prepared pan. Place pan in larger pan and surround halfway up with hot water. Bake in 350 oven 50 minutes. Cake will look like a brownie on top and puff up slightly. Let cool 10 minutes. Invert onto serving platter and rap to remove from pan. Peel off wax paper and cool completely. May be served as is or frosted. (At the restaurant Ruth serves this with espresso crème anglaise or raspberry puree. It can also be frosted with chocolate cream cheese frosting.) Stores well in refrigerator for up to a week. Should be served at room temperature. Freezes well.

Chocolate cream cheese frosting:

1 8-ounce package cream cheese, softened
1 stick unsalted butter, softened
1 pound confectioners sugar
3/4 cup Dutch process cocoa
   (use regular cocoa if you can't get Dutch process)
1 teaspoon vanilla

Combine all ingredients in work bowl of food processor and blend well.

Serves 12.

Santa's North Pole Pumpkin Roll

Leave this dessert out for Santa!

Cake:

3 eggs
1 cup pumpkin
1 cup sugar
3/4 teaspoon lemon juice
3/4 cup flour
1 teaspoon baking powder
2 teaspoons cinnamon
3/4 teaspoon ginger
1/2 teaspoon nutmeg
1/2 teaspoon salt

Filling:

1 cup powdered sugar
8 ounce package cream cheese, softened
1 teaspoon vanilla
4 tablespoons butter, softened

Beat eggs on medium speed 4-5 minutes. Add sugar gradually. Add pumpkin and lemon juice. Beat additional minute. Sift dry ingredients together and slowly add to pumpkin mixture, mix until well-blended.

Spread into a greased 15 x 10 x 1 inch pan lined with waxed paper. If desired, 1/2 cup chopped nuts can be added over top. Bake at 375 degrees for 15 minutes. Turn out on a towel, roll up cake and towel together like a jellyroll. When cake is cooled, unroll and spread filling over cake. Re-roll and chill before serving. When ready to serve, sift additional powdered sugar lightly over top.

Serves 6 – 8.

White Chocolate Coeur a la Crème

Bramble Inn & Restaurant
Brewster, MA
Chef/Owner Ruth Manchester

"One of our most sought-after desserts, this recipe has appeared in 'Bon Appetit,' 'Gourmet,' 'The New York Times,' 'Chocolatier,' and most recently in 'The Naples Daily News.' A real hit on Valentine's Day, but delicious anytime." – Ruth

Ingredients:

8 ounces cream cheese
4 ounces white chocolate
3/4 cup confectioners sugar
1½ cups heavy cream

Melt chocolate and combine in Cuisinart with cream cheese and sugar. Beat cream stiff. Fold cheese mixture thoroughly into cream. Line individual heart-shaped molds, or one large mold, with dampened cheesecloth and fill each mold to top with mixture. Fold cheesecloth over top, cover, and chill 6 hours.

Note: To serve, unmold onto plate lined with strawberry coulis. Remove cheesecloth and garnish with whipped cream, mint sprig, and sliced strawberry. (Ruth also sweetens and thins a little sour cream, places it in a squeeze bottle, and makes little drops on top of the coulis. She then draws a knife through them to form more hearts.)

Serves 12.

French Chocolate Pie

My grandmother, Irene Jasper, used to make this dessert for the holidays. In my opinion, it is the best chocolate pie on earth!

Ingredients:

1 8-inch baked pie shell
1/2 cup butter
3/4 cup sugar
2 squares unsweetened chocolate, melted
1 teaspoon vanilla
2 eggs

Cream butter, gradually add sugar, creaming well. Blend in melted and thoroughly cooled chocolate and vanilla.

Add eggs, one at a time. After each egg is added to the mixture, beat for 5 minutes on medium speed with electric mixer.

Chill at least 2 hours. Top with whipped cream.

Serves 8.

Christmas Eve Pecan Pie

My wife's pecan pie. Marital Bliss!

Ingredients:

1 cup white corn syrup
1 cup dark brown sugar
1/8 teaspoon salt
1/3 cup melted butter
3 eggs, slightly beaten
1 teaspoon vanilla
1 heaping cup whole pecans

Combine syrup, sugar, salt, and butter. Mix well. Add vanilla and eggs. Mix until eggs are well blended into mixture. Mix in pecans and pour into 9-inch unbaked crust. Bake 45 – 55 minutes at 350 until set, but still jiggles slightly in the center.

Serves 8.

Rum Cake with Holiday Sauce

Honeysuckle Hill Bed & Breakfast
West Barnstable, MA

Ingredients:

1 package yellow cake mix with pudding
1 cup sour cream
1/3 cup vegetable oil
1/4 cup rum
3 eggs

Preheat over to 350 degrees. Grease and flour two 9-inch cake pans. In a large bowl combine all ingredients at low speed on mixer until well blended. Then beat two minutes at high speed. Pour into pans and bake 25 to 35 minutes until done. Cool on rack for 15 minutes. Remove from pans.

Sauce:

1 can cherry pie filling
1 can whole cranberry sauce
1/2 cup rum

When ready to serve, heat pie filling and cranberry sauce in a large skillet just until mixture comes to a boil. Pour rum over hot fruit. DO NOT STIR. Ignite with match. Ladle flaming fruit over cake wedges.

Serves 16.

Sandwich Glass Pie

Deming Jarves, founder of the Boston & Sandwich Glass Company, would have loved this one!

Ingredients:

3 packages of Jell-O (red, purple, and green)
1/4 cup cold water
1 package unflavored gelatin
1 cup pineapple juice
1 pint all-purpose cream
1 teaspoon vanilla
1/2 cup sugar

Crust:
1½ cups vanilla wafers crushed fine
4 tablespoons melted butter
1/4 teaspoon cinnamon
mix well and pat into greased 9-inch springform pan.
reserve 1 tablespoon for top of pie

Prepare the Jell-O packages as directed and put into three 8-inch square pans until jellied. Cut into 1-inch squares. Put all cubes into a bowl to mix colors. Set aside.

Stir cold water and 1 package unflavored gelatin together. Add boiled pineapple juice and stir mixture until it is clear.

Whip cream, vanilla, and sugar until stiff. Add cooled pineapple juice mixture, slowly. Add Jell-O cubes and mix gently. Pour into springform pan. Sprinkle 1 tablespoon of crumb mixture over top.

Pie has to be refrigerated at least six hours before serving. Pie can be made one day ahead. Keep in refrigerator.

Serves 8.

Grapenut Custard

Scargo Café
Dennis, MA

Ingredients:

9 large eggs
1/2 gallon light cream
2 cups sugar
2 tablespoons vanilla extract
1 cup grapenuts
1 teaspoon nutmeg
1 teaspoon cinnamon

Whip eggs, cream, sugar, and vanilla completely with a wire whisk or mixer. Pour mixture into a 9 x 12 inch pan (Scargo uses a stainless-steel pan called a "half hotel pan") and sprinkle grapenuts, cinnamon, and nutmeg evenly over the top. Place the 9 x 12 pan into a large pan to form a water bath (fill with water equal to the height of custard mixture) and place them carefully into a preheated 325-degree oven for approximately 90 minutes.

Chef's Notes:

Oven temperature will greatly affect cooking time, so check for doneness by gently wiggling pan. Remove as soon as center of custard mixture begins to gel. Cool at room temperature and serve warm or chilled, topped with whipped cream and lightly sprinkled with cinnamon sugar.

Serves 12 – 13.

Cranberry Mincemeat Pie*

The Flume Restaurant
Mashpee, MA

Ingredients:

Pastry for 9-inch double crust
2 cups mincemeat
2 cups whole cranberry sauce
1 apple, peeled, cored and chopped

Preheat oven to 450 degrees. Line a pie plate with half of the pastry dough. Combine cranberry, mincemeat and apple. Turn into pie shell. Make a lattice top.

Bake 10 minutes at 450 degrees. Reduce heat to 350 degrees and bake for an additional 25 minutes.

Serves 8.

*Excerpted from Cape Cod Wampanoag Cookbook, Wampanoag Indian Recipes, Images & Lore by Chief Earl Mills, Published by Clear Light Publishing, www.clearlightbooks.com.

Jack Frost's Carrot Cake

This is a rich, decadent carrot cake that my mother, Marilyn Jasper, has been making for years.

Ingredients:

2 cups flour
2 cups sugar
1¼ cups vegetable oil
1/4 cup sour cream
3 eggs, slightly beaten
2 teaspoons baking soda
1 teaspoon salt
1 cup raisins
4-5 ounces flaked coconut
1 small can crushed pineapple, slightly drained
2 cups grated carrots
3/4 cups chopped nuts
2 teaspoons cinnamon
2 teaspoons vanilla

Combine sugar, eggs, and oil in large bowl of electric mixer. Beat on medium-low speed. Sift all dry ingredients and add to egg mixture, beat until mixed. Add remaining ingredients and mix by hand until well blended. Pour into two 9-inch cake pans, well greased. Line bottom of pans with wax paper. Bake at 350 degrees 45 – 50 minutes, or until toothpick comes out clean. Let cake sit in pan at least 20 minutes. Remove carefully, as this is a very tender cake.

Cool before frosting.

Frosting:

1 stick softened butter
1 8-ounce package cream cheese, room temperature
1 box confectioners sugar
1 teaspoon vanilla

Blend cream cheese and butter in mixer, add sugar and vanilla. Beat until smooth.

Serves 10 – 12.

Cranberry Betty

From the Cape Cod Mixing Bowl Cookbook

Ingredients:

2 cups cranberries
1 cup sugar
1 cup water
2½ cups vanilla wafer crumbs
1/2 cup finely chopped walnuts
2 tablespoons butter

Cook cranberries, sugar, and water about 10 minutes or until skins begin to break. Mix crumbs and nuts and sprinkle about 1/3 of the mixture on the bottom of a thickly buttered 1½ quart baking dish. Cover with half the cranberries, dot with butter, and sprinkle with half the remaining crumbs. Repeat the layers. Bake at 375 degrees for 25 to 30 minutes, until top is browned. Serve warm or cold with whipped cream or ice cream.

Serves 4 – 6.

Centerville Apricot and Date Fruitcake

This is one of the chunkiest, most delicious fruitcakes I've ever tasted. My grandmother, Dora Lederman, used to make this at her home in Centerville.

Ingredients:

3 eggs
1½ teaspoons vanilla
1 heaping tablespoon sour cream
3/4 cup plus one tablespoon flour
3/4 cup packed brown sugar
1/4 teaspoon baking soda
1/4 teaspoon baking powder
dash of salt
2 cups whole pecans or walnuts
1 8-ounce package whole apricots
2 cups dates, cut into quarters
1 cup raisins
1 cup candied red cherries cut in half

Beat the eggs, vanilla and sour cream. Set aside. In large bowl sift the flour and all the dry ingredients. Add fruit and mix well. Add egg mixture and coat well.

Pour into loaf pan (3¼ x 12 inch pan) lined with greased wax paper and bake about 1 hour at 325 degrees.

Serves 10.

Trafalgar Squares

The Dunbar Tea Shop
Sandwich, MA
Chef/Bakers Teresa Keough, Paula Hegarty

Ingredients:

8 ounces cream cheese, softened
3 eggs
3/4 cup water
2 cups flour
1 teaspoon baking soda
12 ounces chocolate chips
2⅓ cups sugar
1/2 cup margarine
1½ ounces unsweetened chocolate squares
1/2 cup sour cream
1/4 teaspoon salt

Preheat oven to 375. Grease and flour a 9 x 13 inch pan.

Combine cream cheese and 1/3 cup sugar until well blended. Add 1 egg and mix well. Put aside.

In a separate bowl combine 1/2 cup margarine, water, and chocolate squares in pan over moderate heat until melted.

Mix 2 cups sugar, 2 eggs, flour, baking soda, sour cream, salt, and melted chocolate until well blended. Pour into prepared pan. Spoon cream cheese mix over chocolate batter, swirl with a knife. Sprinkle with 6 ounces chocolate chips. Bake 35 – 40 minutes. Cool completely.

Make a glaze by melting together the remaining 6 ounces chocolate chips and 1/2 stick margarine spread evenly over squares, sprinkle with chocolate flakes, and slice.

Serves 12.

Scottish Shortbread

The Dunbar Tea Shop
Sandwich, MA
Chef/Bakers Teresa Keough, Paula Hegarty

Ingredients:

4 ounces butter, softened
2 ounces sugar
6 ounces flour

Preheat oven to 325°. Grease
and flour a 7-inch round tin. Mix all
ingredients together. Press evenly into prepared tin.
Using fork tines, press around the edges, and then prick the
shortbread a few times. Bake for 35 – 40 minutes until firm and
golden. Cut immediately into 8 triangles. Sprinkle with extra sugar.

Spicy Pumpkin Bread

Maureen Hampsch – Woodill

A delicious, flavorful pumpkin bread.

Ingredients:

4 cups flour
3 cups sugar
4 eggs, beaten
1 cup oil
1 can pumpkin mix (30 oz.)
1 teaspoon allspice
1 teaspoon nutmeg
1 teaspoon cinnamon
1½ teaspoons ground cloves
1 teaspoon pumpkin pie spice
1 teaspoon baking powder
2 teaspoons baking soda
1½ teaspoons salt
1/2 cup Grapenuts
1/3 cup water

Combine all ingredients in a bowl. Mix well. Pour into greased loaf pan.
Bake at 350° for approximately 50 – 60 minutes.

Serves 8.

Sweet Potato Pie

Ingredients:

2 cans (16 oz) sweet potatoes, drained
2 cups light cream
1 cup plus 1 tablespoon packed brown sugar
4 tablespoons butter, melted
1½ teaspoons vanilla
1¼ teaspoons cinnamon
1/2 teaspoon nutmeg
1/2 teaspoon ginger
1/2 teaspoon salt
3 large eggs

Use your favorite piecrust for one-crust pie

Beat sweet potatoes and melted butter until smooth, add cream and remaining ingredients. Beat until well blended. Pour into unbaked crust in a greased 9-inch pie plate.

Bake 40 minutes at 350 or until knife inserted comes out clean (check after 35 minutes). Serve warm or refrigerate.

Optional: 1 cup heavy cream, 1 tablespoon sugar, and 1 teaspoon bourbon. Beat until soft peaks form. Serve alongside pie.

Serves 8.

Plantation Gingerbread

The Cranberry Inn of Chatham
Chatham, MA

Ingredients:

1 cup butter, softened
1 cup sugar
3 eggs
1 cup molasses
3/4 cup hot water
2½ cups all-purpose flour
1 teaspoon baking soda
1½ teaspoon ground ginger
1 teaspoon cinnamon
1/2 teaspoon nutmeg
1/2 teaspoon salt
2 tablespoons confectioners sugar & additional nutmeg to taste

Preheat oven to 350 degrees.

Cream butter and sugar. Add eggs one at a time and beat well. Gradually add molasses and hot water. Combine all dry ingredients. Gradually add to wet mixture on low until well combined. Pour batter into greased 13 x 9 x 2 inch pan. Bake for 30 – 35 minutes. Cool on rack, sprinkle with confectioners sugar and nutmeg, slice and enjoy!

Gingerbread Cookies

Bramble Inn & Restaurant
Brewster, MA
Chef/Owner Ruth Manchester

Ingredients:

4 cups unbleached flour
2 tablespoons cocoa powder
5 teaspoons ginger
2 teaspoons cinnamon
1 teaspoon cloves
1 teaspoon baking soda
1 teaspoon salt
2 sticks unsalted butter or
   shortening, softened
1 cup sugar
1 egg lightly beaten
1/2 cup molasses

Beat sugar and shortening or butter until light. Add egg and molasses. Combine dry ingredients and add to creamed mixture a little at a time. Knead dough a few minutes. Divide into four parts, wrap and chill. Preheat oven to 350°. Roll onto lightly floured surface. Shape and bake on greased and floured sheet pans 15 to 20 minutes depending upon thickness.

Christmas Brunch

Bramble Inn Baked Fruited French Toast

Bramble Inn & Restaurant
Brewster, MA
Chef/Owner Ruth Manchester

"This is a wonderful 'do-ahead' Christmas morning treat that will let you open presents while breakfast cooks." – Ruth

Ingredients:

4 cups cubed day-old homemade bread
2 apples cut in 1/4 inch dice or 1½ cups berries
8 ounces cream cheese
8 eggs
2 cups milk
1½ teaspoons cinnamon
1 teaspoon vanilla
3 tablespoons sugar
powdered sugar

Place bread in a large bowl. Combine eggs and cream cheese in Cuisinart and process smooth. Add sugar, milk, vanilla, and cinnamon and process again to combine. Pour over bread cubes. Add fruit and mix well. Pour into greased lasagna pan. May be kept overnight up to this point or baked in 400 degree oven 30 – 35 minutes. Dust top with powdered sugar and serve with maple syrup.

Serves 12.

Crème Caramel French Toast

Village Green Inn
Falmouth, MA

Ingredients:

2 tablespoons corn syrup
1 cup brown sugar
1/4 cup butter
1½ pounds cinnamon raisin bread
6 eggs
2 cups milk
2 cups light cream
1/3 cup sugar
1 tablespoon vanilla
1/2 teaspoon salt
sour cream

Preparation:

In a saucepan combine corn syrup, brown sugar, and butter, and melt until smooth and bubbly. Spread on 11 x 17 inch glass baking dish. Overlap bread like dominoes on the syrup. In large bowl combine eggs, milk, cream, sugar, vanilla, and salt. Pour over bread. Cover with foil.

Refrigerate overnight. Bake at 350 degrees, covered, 50 – 55 minutes uncovering last 10 minutes. The toast should be puffy and golden. Cut into 8 or 10 pieces and invert to serve.

Top each piece with 2 tablespoons sour cream and accompany with fresh berries or a cranberry or raspberry sauce.

Serves 8 – 10.

Dutch Apple French Toast

The Dunbar Tea Shop
Sandwich, MA
Chef/Bakers Teresa Keough, Paula Hegarty

Ingredients:

3/4 cup butter
3 tablespoons dark corn syrup
1 loaf cinnamon raisin bread
1 quart milk
1½ cups brown sugar
4 apples, peeled, cored and sliced
8 eggs
1½ teaspoons vanilla

Heat the sugar, butter, and corn syrup until syrupy. Pour into 10 x 15 inch pan. Spread apples over syrup. Cut the crusts off the bread and layer the slices of bread over the apples. Beat the remaining ingredients together and pour the mixture over the bread. Refrigerate overnight. Bake at 350 for 45 minutes.

Serves 10 – 12.

Dora's Holiday Cheese Blintzes

Dora Lederman

My grandmother's secret recipe.

Ingredients:

1¾ cups water
1/4 cup milk
2 eggs
2 cups flour
1 teaspoon melted butter
pinch of salt

Beat all ingredients in a blender or electric mixer until smooth. Grease a small fry pan with a small amount of butter, heat until hot (but not smoky). Drop 3 tablespoons of batter into fry pan, tipping pan to spread batter thin. Cook about 2 minutes or until lightly browned. Turn cooked blintzes onto a thin dish towel, brown side up. Continue until batter is used. Use a paper towel with small amount of butter on it to grease fry pan each time you put batter into fry pan.

Filling:
3/4 pound farmers cheese
3/4 pound cream cheese
1 teaspoon sugar
salt and pepper to taste
1 egg

Mix the filling in an electric mixer until smooth.

Put 2 tablespoons filling into each blintz. Fold the sides over and then roll. Fry in butter on both sides until lightly brown and filling is hot.

Serve with sour cream. Stewed blueberries can be served over the sour cream.

Oven Shirred Eggs

The Dunbar Tea Shop
Sandwich, MA
Chef/Bakers Teresa Keough, Paula Hegarty

Ingredients:

6 eggs
12 tablespoons half-and-half
1 cup grated cheese

Preheat oven to 450°. Spray six muffin tins with non-stick spray. Break one egg into each cup. Pour 2 tablespoons half-and-half over each. Sprinkle with grated cheese. Bake for 8 minutes. Carefully lift eggs from cups with spoon. Serve over toast or on top of English muffin.

Cinnamon Scones

The Colonial House Inn
Yarmouth Port, MA
Executive Chef Ivan Velinov

Ingredients:

2 cups flour
1/3 cup sugar
1 teaspoon baking powder
1 teaspoon cinnamon
1/4 teaspoon salt
1/2 cup butter
2/3 cup milk
1 egg, beaten
1 teaspoon vanilla

Heat oven to 400 degrees. Combine flour, sugar, baking powder, cinnamon, and salt. Using pastry blender or fork, cut in butter until mixture resembles coarse crumbs. Combine milk, egg, and vanilla. Add to flour mixture, stirring until dry ingredients are moistened. With floured hands, shape dough into 8-inch round on ungreased cookie sheet. Sprinkle with additional sugar, if desired. Cut dough into 8 wedges; slightly separate the wedges. Bake at 400 degrees for 15 to 20 minutes. Serve warm.

VARIATIONS:
Orange Cinnamon Scones: Add 1 teaspoon grated orange peel to dry ingredients.
Gingerbread Scones: Add 1 teaspoon ginger to dry ingredients and 2 teaspoons molasses to liquid ingredients.

Serves 8.

Strawberry Bread

Marilyn Jasper

This tasty bread will enhance any Christmas brunch.

Ingredients:

1 ½ cups flour
1 teaspoon baking soda
1 teaspoon powder
3/4 teaspoon cinnamon
1 cup sugar
1/3 cup butter
3/4 teaspoon salt
2 eggs
1/2 cup water
1/2 cup chopped walnuts
2 pints strawberries, plus 1/2 cup
1 teaspoon vanilla

Put one cup of pureed strawberries in small saucepan and heat to boiling over medium heat. Cook one minute, stirring constantly. Cool mixture. Slice the remaining strawberries (take out 1/4 cup and set aside) and add to chilled pureed strawberries. Set aside.

Sift dry ingredients into a large mixing bowl. Set aside. Cream butter and sugar until fluffy, add eggs and beat until well blended, add vanilla. Add half the flour mixture and then half the water into the creamed mixture beating on low speed until all the flour and water is blended. Stir in the strawberries and walnuts.

Pour batter into greased 9 x 5 inch loaf pan. Place the 1/4 cup sliced strawberries on top of batter. (Put greased wax paper on bottom of pan so it won't stick). Bake about 50 – 60 minutes at 350 degrees until toothpick comes out clean. If bread is getting too brown, cover top with foil.

Note: For a more intense strawberry flavor, 1/2 to 1 teaspoon pure strawberry extract can be added to the batter.

Serve with strawberry cream cheese if desired.

Serves 8.

Cranberry-Walnut Morning Cake

Village Green Inn
Falmouth, MA

Ingredients:

1 stick butter
1 cup sugar
2 eggs
1 teaspoon baking powder
1 teaspoon baking soda
2 cups flour
1/2 teaspoon salt
1/2 pint sour cream
1 teaspoon almond extract
1 large can cranberry sauce (whole berry)
1 cup chopped walnuts

Cream together butter, sugar, and eggs. Blend together baking powder, baking soda, flour, and salt. Stir flour mixture into cream mixture, alternating with sour cream. Fold in extract and nuts. Pour half the batter into a greased tube pan. Spread half can of cranberry sauce on top of batter. Pour in rest of batter, top with remaining cranberry sauce.

Bake at 350° for 50 – 60 minutes. Allow to cool before removing from the pan.

Topping:

Mix together 3/4 cups of confectioners sugar, 1/2 teaspoon almond extract, and add enough warm water so you can drizzle onto warm cake with spoon.

Serves 16.

Rachel's Banana Bread

Rachel Boylestad

Ingredients:

2 large ripe bananas, mashed
2 eggs, slightly beaten
1¾ cups flour, sifted
1¼ cups sugar
1/2 cup vegetable oil
1/4 cup sour cream
1 teaspoon baking soda
2 teaspoons vanilla
1/2 teaspoon salt

Grease 9 x 5 inch loaf pan. Sift flour, baking soda, and salt. Set aside. Combine eggs, oil, bananas, sugar, and vanilla in a mixer. Beat on low speed about 1 minute. Blend in flour mixture and sour cream. Slowly beat until blended about 1 – 2 minutes. Pour into pan and bake 1 hour and 15 minutes at 325 degrees.

Serves 8.

Cliff's Blueberry Muffins

Bramble Inn & Restaurant
Brewster, MA
Chef/Owner Ruth Manchester

"Cliff makes these wonderful and easy muffins every Christmas at the inn. He uses frozen Maine blueberries that we picked in August at my nephew's farm in Maine." – Ruth

Ingredients:

1 stick melted butter
3/4 cup sugar
2 eggs
2 cups flour
2 teaspoons baking powder
3/4 cup milk
1 teaspoon vanilla
2 cups blueberries
1/4 cup sugar (for muffin tops)

Beat butter, sugar, and eggs. Combine dry ingredients and add to mixture. Add milk and stir to combine. Fold in blueberries. Line muffin pan with paper muffin cups. Fill each cup 1/2 full. Sprinkle with remaining sugar and bake in 400 degree oven for about 20 minutes.

Serves 12.

Cranberry Marmalade

Green Briar Jam Kitchen
Sandwich, MA

Ingredients:

1 grapefruit
1 orange
1/2 lemon
3 cups cranberries
3 cups water
5 cups sugar

Cut ends from grapefruit, orange, and lemon. Cut each in half length-wise. Cut each half into three lengthwise wedges. Remove center pith and slice each wedge crosswise into thin wedges. Place in pan and add water.

Cook over low heat for 20 minutes. Add cranberries and sugar and cook until thick. Pour into sterilized jars and seal.

Yield : 6 eight-ounce jars.

For Additional Recipes:

www.oncapepublications.com

Other Books from On Cape Publications

Haunted Cape Cod & the Islands by Mark Jasper

Haunted Inns of New England by Mark Jasper

In the Footsteps of Thoreau: 25 Historic & Nature Walks by Adam Gamble

Walking the Shores of Cape Cod by Elliott Carr

The Blizzard of '78 by Michael Tougias

Baseball by the Beach: A History of America's National Pastime on Cape Cod by Christopher Price

Quabbin: A History & Explorer's Guide by Michael Tougias

Sea Stories of Cape Cod & the Islands by Admont G. Clark

Cape Cod (Audio) by Henry David Thoreau

Coloring Cape Cod, Martha's Vineyard & Nantucket by James Owens

Cape Cod Light: The Lighthouse at Dangerfield by Paul Giambarba

1880 Atlas of Barnstable Country: Cape Cod's Earliest Atlas edited by Adam Gamble

Howie Schneider Unshucked: A Cartoon Collection about the Cape, the Country and Life Itself by Howie Schneider

Penikese Island of Hope by Thomas Buckley

A Guide to Nature on Cape Cod & the Islands edited by Greg O'Brien

Windmills of New England by Dan Lombardo

Cape Cod, Massachusetts